AMERICAN INDIAN GAMES

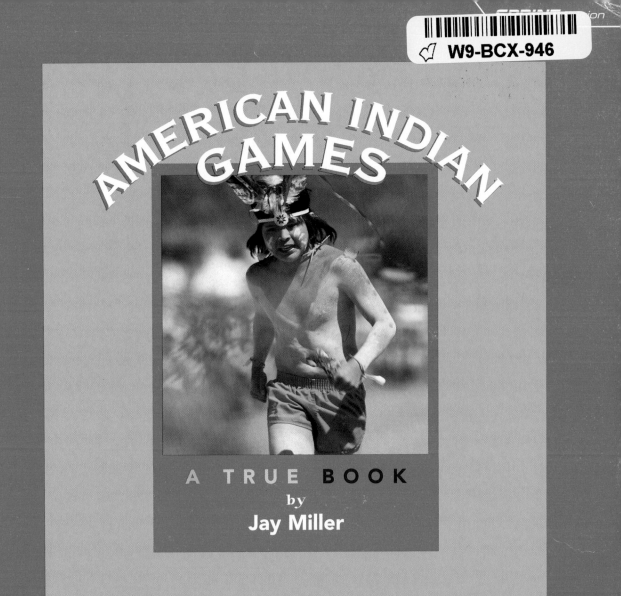

A TRUE BOOK

by

Jay Miller

SCHOLASTIC INC.

New York Toronto London Auckland Sydney
Mexico City New Delhi Hong Kong Buenos Aires

For help in reading and writing these books, Jay Miller thanks Zachary, Vi, and Rebecca.

Reading Consultant
Linda Cornwell
Learning Resource Consultant
Indiana Department of
Education

Choctaw lacrosse players stretch for the ball.

Copyright © 2003, 1996 by Children's Press, a division of Grolier Publishing Co., Inc.
All rights reserved. Published by Scholastic Inc., 557 Broadway, New York, NY 10012.
Printed in the U.S.A.

ISBN 0-516-24581-3

SCHOLASTIC and associated logos and designs are trademarks and/or registered trademarks of Scholastic Inc.

1 2 3 4 5 6 7 8 9 10 61 12 11 10 09 08 07 06 05 04 03

Contents

An Inuit girl today enjoys baseball in northern Canada.

Why Play Games?

People everywhere play games. They play for many reasons. Games are fun! Plus, games build strong bodies. But games also teach. Games teach about sharing. And they teach about taking turns.

American Indians felt that games must be played the right way. Tsimshian Indians live in British Columbia, Canada. They tell a story. It's about children who made too much noise while playing.

Once there was a town where noisy children played. It made Heaven angry. So Heaven sent a feather to float above the town.

The children tried to grab the feather. They stood on each other's shoulders. The chief's son grabbed it. But he could not let go. The others became stuck to him. They slowly rose into the air. They

This boy is practicing with a bow and arrow.

were never seen again.

Games helped American Indians stay alive. Many Indians hunted animals with bows and arrows. So the boys played with toy bows and arrows. They would shoot at

Hopi boys shoot arrows through a hoop, almost 90 years ago.

targets. They would roll a
hoop. Then they would try
shooting an arrow through it.
It wasn't easy. But it taught
them good aim.

Arctic Ocean

Inuit

Inuit

Copper
Inuit

Inuit

Northwest

Tsimshian

Pacific Ocean

Makah

Plains

Lakota   Cheyenne

Oglala

Sauk   Iroquois

Potawatomi   Mohawk

Delaware

Atlantic Ocean

Southwest

Hopi Zuni

Southeast

Choctaw

NORTH AMERICAN
TRIBES

Gulf of Mexico

Caribbean Sea

Toys

American Indian children
played with many kinds
of toys.

Most girls had dolls. In the
East, some dolls were made
from corn husks. Some were
made of mud or deerskin.
They had no faces. Lakota girls
played house with small tipis.

Toys a Lakota child might have used (top); a carefully made doll—with no face (bottom left); Oglala girls play with tipis in the 1890s (bottom right).

"Jabber" toys could be made in many different ways.

Boys didn't just shoot arrows. They had other games, too. Jabber was one. The jabber was a stick. On one end it was pointed. At the other end was a string. Hanging on the string were some objects. Players tried to hook the objects on the stick. This game kept eyes and hands working together. It took skill.

In places like the Northwest, people traveled by water. Children who lived there had small canoes. Children learned how to paddle and how to stay safe in the water.

In the Plains it often snowed. Then children went sledding. Their sleds were made of buffalo ribs! The ribs were tied together. The children slid down hills. Sometimes they ended the trip on frozen streams. On the ice they slid far.

This sled was made from buffalo ribs.

Just for Fun

People of all ages played games. They weren't just for kids. Everyone liked to make patterns with string. They wrapped it around their fingers. One pattern looked like a cradle. That's why the game was called cat's cradle. People still play it today.

16

Cat's cradle is played in northwestern Canada (above) and the southwestern United States.

Women played with dice. They made dice from fruit pits or wood. Sometimes they used bone or beaver teeth. Each side

These women are playing a dice game (above). This is a Potawatomi bowl and dice (top right). These are Cheyenne dice and their carrying bag (bottom right).

had different colors and marks. The marks were dark lines or dots. The marks stood for points. The dice were tossed in a basket or wooden bowl. If all dice landed the same way, the

18

player got extra points.

Men played a guessing game. They took four moccasins. Then they took something small. It might be a nut. One team hid the nut under one shoe. The other team had to guess where it was.

Under which moccasin is the nut hiding?

Preparing for Life

Games were part of growing up. Some tribes had baby talk words that made everyone laugh. Some tribes made up tongue twisters. They were hard to say. It was good practice. It taught people to speak carefully.

Everywhere, girls played house. They did what older

An Inuit teenager learns how to make bannock, a kind of bread.

women did. They cooked and cleaned. On the Plains, they pretended to cut up buffalo meat. Near the Rockies, they looked for seeds. Then they roasted them.

Boys played sports to grow strong. They learned to wrestle. Teams pretended to be enemies. They had snowball fights. When it was warm, they would use mud balls. Sometimes it hurt. They learned to live with the pain. In some games, they went without food and water. They got bruises and cuts. But they didn't complain. They were learning to be brave.

Young Mohawks of today train in a survival school (top). Here's a canoe race in British Columbia (bottom).

In the Northwest, men had canoe races. They used canoes made for war. Each one held twelve people. It was good practice. It kept them ready for battle.

Young and old men tested their strength. They would lift heavy rocks. Then they would try to carry them. Some rocks were painted. Others had designs chipped into them.

In winter, men or boys played another game. It was called snowsnake. They carved a line in snow or ice. Then they took turns throwing a spear along the line. The spear was ten feet long! Whoever threw the spear the farthest won.

Part of a Team

Some Indian nations farmed.
They lived in large villages.
People there played team games.

In the Southwest, men played
a game that's like soccer. They
kicked a round stone across the
desert. The first team to kick
their stone over the goal line won.
The stone was hard. So, Hopi

men grew a long, curved toenail. This kept their big toe from getting hurt.

In the East, tribes made up another game. It was called lacrosse or stickball. People now play this game all over the world.

Each lacrosse player has a

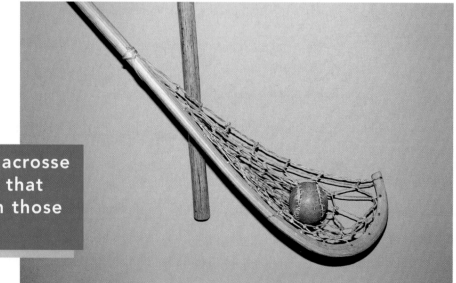

Old Iroquois lacrosse sticks are not that different from those used today.

Children practice lacrosse skills.

racket. The racket is a stick with a net on the top. Iroquois use only one racket. That's how most people play. The Choctaw use two rackets. They hold one in each hand. Players try to catch a three-inch ball in the net. The ball is made of wood or

Choctaw lacrosse players use two rackets.

deerskin stuffed with hair. Then they try to carry the ball across the goal line. In big games, hundreds of men would play.

People tell an old tale about lacrosse. This is what they say. In the first game, animals played against birds. At first, neither team wanted the bat.

But the animals took him. The bat could run and fly. So, the animals won. Since then, Choctaw players ask the bat for help. Sometimes they wear something from a bat. They consider it lucky.

Choctaw players still dress in special ways for luck. Some will play in bare feet. Others wear a necklace of horsehair. That's because horses run fast. They also ask people to pray for them. They believe that it is good to be brave and strong.

But that's not enough. They want to get help from the spirits, too.

Women in many tribes played shinny. This game is like field hockey. Each player used a stick with a curved end. They hit a ball along the ground. The ball was made of wood or stuffed leather.

The Makah in the Northwest played shinny with two curved sticks. One was for hitting the ball. The other was for carrying it to the goal. They usually played after one of their leaders killed a

Shinny is still played in Arizona. And it's still popular.

whale. The whale was brought to the beach. There was a feast. Everyone ate. Then they played shinny. They used a soft whale bone as the ball. Some American Indians still play shinny today.

Special Games

Some games were special. The Delaware played a ball game in the summer. They believed it would help their crops grow.

Men played against women. The game was part soccer and part football. The men could only kick the ball. The women could only throw it. The ball was made of leather stuffed with deer hair. They played on a long field. The field had goals at either end. The goals had two posts. To win, a team had to take the ball through the goal posts.

The game was a prayer. It was for Corn Mother and the crops. In summer, they played. And the crops grew. In the fall, they stopped. Then the crops were ready to harvest.

Games were sometimes used to stop fights. For example, Copper Inuit in Canada held singing duels. The songs made fun of the other person. A crowd listened. The person with the funnier song won.

In 1906, the Hopi town of Oraibi had a problem. People were not getting along. They didn't fight. They held a tug of war instead. Both teams pulled against each other.

A song duel may be happening in this Inuit gathering.

One team pulled the other over a line in the sand. The losing team had to leave town. Today, these groups still live apart.

The Bone Game

The Spanish came to California. They brought the bone game with them. Indians learned it. They called this game lahal. They taught it to other tribes. People in the West still play this guessing game. Two teams sit across from each other. A person on one team has two bone tubes. One is plain. The other has a black band. The person puts one tube in each fist.

The other team sings and drums. One person from that team guesses which hand has the plain bone. To make a guess, the person points at one fist or the other.

The teams count the number of correct guesses. They use sticks to keep score. When one team wins all twelve sticks, that side wins. Then they play again.

New Games

Europeans brought other games. They brought checkers, dominos, and chess. Indians enjoyed these games. They carved game pieces from wood or stone. Some used bone or ivory. Playing boards were made of leather, wood, and stone.

Indians also learned card

Men play dominos on Standing Rock Reservation in the 1930s.

games. They bought cards from traders. They made their own cards, too. They used leather or bark.

Eskimos carved dominos from ivory. They drilled the holes. Then they painted the dots by hand.

American Indian Games Today

Today, American Indian children enjoy all kinds of sports. Track and field is popular. Baseball, football, and basketball are, too. Many Indian schools have won awards in these sports.

Jim Thorpe was a famous

Two American Indian junior-high football teams are playing in New Mexico (top). A Zuni Pueblo high-school cross-country team competes (bottom).

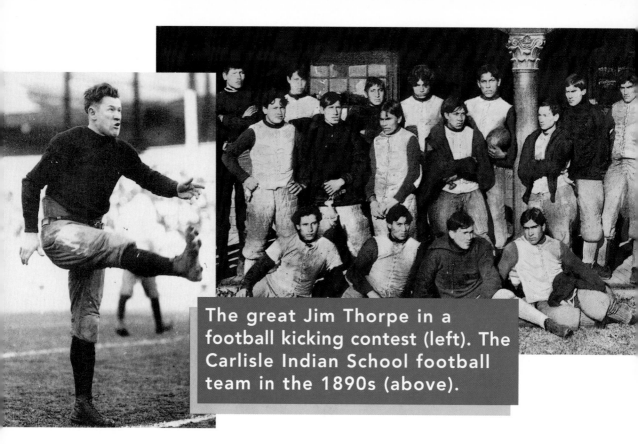

The great Jim Thorpe in a football kicking contest (left). The Carlisle Indian School football team in the 1890s (above).

athlete. He was also a Sauk from Oklahoma. He played football and baseball for the Carlisle Indian School in Pennsylvania. He was on their track-and-field team, too. He won gold medals in the 1912 Summer Olympics.

American Indians today play all kinds of sports well. But canoe racing, lacrosse, and lahal stay popular. These games are part of a rich tradition. And they are still fun.

To Find Out More

Here are more places to learn about American Indian games:

 **Books**

 **Organizations**

Bierhorst, John, ed. **Lightning Inside You, and Other Native American Riddles.** William Morrow and Company, 1993.

Bierhorst, John, ed. **The Sacred Path: Spells, Prayers, and Power Songs of the American Indians.** William Morrow and Company, 1983.

Blood, Charles L. **American Indian Games and Crafts.** Franklin Watts, 1981.

Crum, Robert. **Eagle Drum: On the Powwow Trail with a Young Grass Dancer.** Four Winds Press, 1994.

American Indian Athletic Hall of Fame
Haskell Indian Junior
 College
Lawrence, KS 66044

National Museum of the American Indian
Smithsonian Institution
470 L'Enfant Plaza SW
Suite 7103, MRC 934
Washington, DC 20560
Runner@IC.SI.EDU

National Park Service
Office of Public Inquiries
P.O. Box 37127
Washington, DC 20013
(202) 208-4747
http://www.nps.gov

The Southwest Museum
234 Museum Drive
Los Angeles, CA 90065
(213) 221-2164
swmuseum@annex.com

Online Sites

A Guide to the Great Sioux Nation
http://www.state.sd.us/state /executive/tourism/sioux/ sioux.htm

Explore landmarks, legends, art, powwows, and other interesting traditions of the Sioux Nation.

National Museum of the American Indian
http://www.nmai.si.edu

Part of the Smithsonian Institution, this online site is filled with interesting facts and exhibits about Western Hemisphere Indians.

Native American Art Gallery
http://www.info1.com/ NAAG/index.html

Browse the catalog of art and artists and sign up for the gallery's newsletter.

Native Web
http://www.nativeweb.org

Discover information about indigenous people all over the world.

Important Words

arrow a stick with feathers on the end and a chipped stone point, it is shot with a bow

bow a flexible piece of wood with a strong cord tied to both ends

canoe a small boat made from a hollowed-out log or from a wooden frame covered with sheets of bark

duel a kind of fight between two people that has special rules

moccasin a soft shoe made of leather

spirit an invisible being with special powers

Index

Meet the Author

Jay Miller lives in Seattle, visiting nearby reservations, mountains, streams, and the Pacific Ocean. He enjoys eating salmon and pie, hiking in the mountains, and kayaking along the shore as much as he enjoys being a writer, professor, and lecturer. He has taught in colleges in the United States and Canada. He belongs to the Delaware Wolf clan. His family is delightful and very complex. He has also authored *American Indian Families*, *American Indian Festivals*, and *American Indian Foods* for the True Book series.